Dark Times Are Over?

Dark Times Are Over?
(A Topical Drama)

Olu Obafemi

UNIVERSITY PRESS PLC
IBADAN
2005

University Press PLC
IBADAN ABA ABUJA AJEGUNLE AKURE BENIN IKEJA ILORIN
JOS KANO MAKURDI ONITSHA OWERRI WARRI ZARIA

© Olu Obafemi 2005

ISBN 978 030 956 X

Printed by Adprint Network Limited, Ibadan
Published by University Press PLC
Three Crowns Building, Jericho, P.M.B. 5095, Ibadan, Nigeria
Fax: 02-2412056 E-mail: unipress@skannet.com
Website: www.universitypressplc.com

Playwright/ Director's Note

The history of *Dark Times Are Over?* began in the year 2000, while I was a Visiting Professor at the young Creative Arts Department of the University of Lagos. It was conceived as a twenty-minute workshop experiment for the 200 level students, led by Segun Adetifa and Stella Damasus-Aboderin—both of whom are now notable superstars in the theatre and movie business world.

In the year 2004, my Advanced Theatre 400 Level class attempted a performance of the fully-developed script for their Theatre Workshop Project—an experiment which persuaded me that it was time to give the play a full-blooded production. A team comprising Dr Sunday Ododo, the Technical Director of *Ajon Players*, Rasheed Abiodun Musa, one of the standing Assistant Directors of the troupe and A.S. Abubakar who has worked and taught with me on all the theatre courses in the Department of English, met several times and arrived at the conclusion that *Ajon Players* should produce the play and utilize one of my pet dreams of starting an inter-disciplinary collaboration in the theatre between the Departments of English and the Performing Arts to realize the play.

The outcome of the whole production process is satisfying and somewhat unique. At audition, a total of two hundred and eight actors, drawn from the two Departments, turned up enthusiastically to pick up a part. This is, in itself amazing, judging from the sensitive nature of the play itself. At the wildest stretch, we were able to take on board some fifty-five actors and sixteen crew members. The remaining cast remained undaunted and attended every rehearsal, which in part became a laboratory experience, as the script continued to wear a new look, on every rehearsal. All the actors and the virtual actors were present in all rehearsals including the technical and dress rehearsal. Picking a slimmer cast that would take the play on the performance engagements was a herculean task. It is a fascinating theatrical experience for all of us.

The premier was also a major event, as it coincided with the first visit of the new Pro-chancellor and Chairman of the Governing Council of the University. The play was adopted as a kind of Command Performance for Prof. Ayo Banjo and his company, the entire University management, led by the Vice-Chancellor, Prof. S.O.O Amali.

The statement of the play is apt in the present state of social incoherence in our educational institutions, over-taken by devious anti-social conducts — ranging from cultism, sexual permissiveness, and examination malpractices and so on — all of these resulting largely from social decadence, a prostrate economy, squalor and ethical rot in the larger society. It is thus a play with a pointed, topical message of genuine relevance to the educational and macro-national system. It is produced as a half-way house between the total theatre form and the modern day agit-prop, laced with campus vernacular register. Every institution producing the play should therefore feel free to utter the campus dialogue and the songs of the various organizations, sects, cults and societies that operate in its environment. The message is unalterable.

Olu Obafemi

Director
May 16, 2005

Dark Times Are Over on Fateful Business

On the fateful afternoon of June 19, 2005, tragedy struck like thunder on a rainless day. The setting was some thirty minutes drive from Ankpa in Kogi State. A cast and crew of thirty-nine, drawn, as a collaborative experiment, of energetic and enthusiastic actors from the English and Performing Arts Departments of the University of Ilorin, under the auspices of my troupe, *Ajon Players*, were heading for the Kogi State College of Education, Ankpa, to stage as Convocation Play, my recently premiered new play (performed on Monday May 16, three days before) *Dark Times Are Over?* Suddenly, the singing and drumming came to an abrupt termination to be replaced by wailing and agony.

A tiny, ram-shackled, over-loaded (with seven passengers) white Tarcel car, on a top mad speed had a tyre-burst, lost total control of the steering and headed straight for the two eighteen-seater buses that conveyed the actors. The first bus managed to swerve off the road and avoided the head-on clash, but it was too late for the second. Then the ghastly smash, which left all eighteen actors in the bus in various states of injury and hurt. The driver of the bus died instantly. Six out of the seven passengers in the death-carrying Tarcel also died instantly. Prompt attention from the host institution at Ankpa, who rushed to the scene and fetched all the victims to the Catholic Hospital Anyigba, followed by total take-over the next day by the University of Ilorin authorities who engaged the medical team of the University of Ilorin Teaching Hospital, ameliorated the extent of mortal casualties. Presently, all the actors have been discharged from the Hospital. Unfortunately, one of the most versatile, multi-talented actors, Adedeji Ariyo Abioye, a 400 level student of the Performing Arts, finally passed on, after frantic efforts by the physicians to save his life.

It is a classic example of the numerous hazards which the theatre business faces in this country—which the playwright Femi Osofisan once aptly described as 'playing dangerously'.

Olu Obafemi

Playwright and Director
July 10, 2005

The Synopsis of *Dark Times Are Over?*

Olu Obafemi's *Dark Times Are Over?* is a social drama that captures, in a profound manner, the anti-social behaviours pervading the Nigerian society, most especially the higher institutions of learning. Coded and crafted in a robust, bold, vitriolic and satiric language and dramaturgy, *Dark Times Are Over?* is also a scathing criticism of the moral degeneration: cultism, prostitution and other social vices, which have turned quite a number of the Nigerian youths into liabilities rather than assets to the Nigerian nation.

Yepa One and Yepa Two are two disgruntled citizens of a fictitious nation called Odaju land. The duo lead a deadly cult group in raping innocent students and recklessly displaying brute force. Beatrice, another party freak and a noted 'half-nude dresser' on campus cannot escape the Yepas, as she is mercilessly raped, thus setting the tone of the conflict of this play.

Placed on a sound total theatre experimental dramatic footing, the timely intervention of the Christian and Muslim groups, the Man O' War, the police men and other positive and progressive social groups at Odaju land combined to collectively rout and arrest the cultists. In the spirit of national rebirth, reorientation and basking in the constant ideology of social transformation also, the old legal system gives way to a new judicial innovativeness called 'The People's Court' (popular referendum) where Agbe, the people's judge, pronounces everybody guilty while condemning Yepa One to twenty-one years imprisonment and calls for the total overhauling and constant re-engineering of the people and the socio-political structures of Odaju land.

Rasheed Abiodun Musa
Assistant Director

Addendum

Thank you very sincerely for watching our play, *Dark Times Are Over?* Remember that all those who support cultism and all anti-social behaviours are themselves instruments and agents of social and cultural dislocations. Let us all, in one breath say 'NO' to cultism and all anti-social behaviours.

A S Abubakar
Assistant Production Manager

Appreciation

The entire production crew and cast of *Dark Times Are Over?* from *Ajon* Players, Departments of English and the Performing Arts express their heart-felt gratitude to the Vice-Chancellor of the University of Ilorin, Professor S.O.O Amali, the University Management, the entire staff and students of Performing Arts and English for their unflinching support towards the success of this production, which is an innovation of inter-disciplinary collaboration in the theatre. Many thanks.

Dr S E Ododo
Production Manager/Technical Director

Dedication

The play is dedicated to the immortal memory of a versatile and highly talented Thespian—Adedeji Ariyo Abioye and the entire cast of the premier production of the play.

CREW MEMBERS

PLAYWRIGHT/DIRECTOR	Olu Obafemi
ASSISTANT DIRECTOR	Rasheed Abiodun Musa
TECHNICAL DIRECTOR/	
PRODUCTION MANAGER	Sunday E. Ododo
ASST. PROD. MANAGER	A.S Abubakar
CHOREOGRAPHERS	Rasheed Abiodun Musa
	Adegboye Yemi
SET DESIGNER	Tosho Awogbami
STAGE MANAGER	Tayo Adeyemi
LIGHTING DESIGNER	Ayo Orija
COSTUME MANAGER	Fatoyinbo Ore-Ofe, Anwana Elizabeth
MAKE-UP ARTISTES	Adetoro Tosin, Binitie O' Seun
PROPS MANAGERS	Adebayo Lawrence, Nnana Francisca
PRODUCTION ASSISTANT	Olumodeji Adeola

CAST

Narrator	- Ojo Moses
Agbe	- Ezekiel Peter
Beatrice	- Ife Toba
Yepa 1	- David Temitope
Yepa 2	- Adebayo Tosin
Lady	- Babalola Titi
Judge	- Labiran Mayowa/Akinriyibi Bola
Prosecutor	- Binitie O'Seun
Porter	- Ajeyomi Victor
Alh. Maikudi	- Ogunjimi Henry
Christian Sisters	- Akinriyibi Bola, Nwachuku Abigail, Ikhayere Gladys, Agboola Christy.
Muslim Brothers	- Ajeyomi Victor, Balogun Adejoke, Olulegan Mojisola, Bolaji Israel
Man 'O' War	- Abioye Adedeji, Babatunde Kadri
Jaycees	- Ibitayo Adedoyin, Akinlabi Silas
Cult Members	- Ebute Susan, Quadri Lanre, Adebayo Lawrence, Fatoyinbo Ore-Ofe, Ogidiagba Sonia.
Aristo Girls	- Ife Toba, Awoyemi Bukola, Esuku Evidence, Olasupo Yvonne.
Kegites	- Otitoju Moses, Adetoro Tosin, Adegboye Yemi, Olaniji Oladotun, Ogunfolu Tope, Anwana Elizabeth, Alao Olufunmi, Olufowobi Tosin.
Policemen	- Akanji Taiwo, Oladipo Kehinde, Ibrahim Abdul, Lanre Quadri, Ogunjimi Henry
Porter	- Ajeyomi Victor
Court Clerk	- Anwana Elizabeth.
MOA	- Oke Aminat, Agboola Christy, Ogungbemi Toluwabori, Ogunjimi Henry, Masanwoola Nike, Adigun Peju.
Court Audience	- Adetoro Tosin, Fatoyinbo Ore-Ofe, Olufowobi Tosin, Ogungbemi Toluwabori, Adeniran Itunu, Olaniji Oladotun, Babatunde Peju, Jimoh Odunayo, Jumoke Faleke.

Dancers	- Agboola Christy, Ogungbemi Toluwabori, Olulegan Mojisola, Adeniji Kemi.
Song Leader	- Faromoniyi Olayinka.
Drummers	- Olalusi Taiwo, Olalusi Kehinde, Oyeniyi Seyi.

SCENE ONE

*(Play opens with a tableau, a dramatic summation of the various situations, episodes and enactments that will constitute the main thrust of the performance beginning with the Kegites. The orchestra raises the Kegites' signature tune, **sanyo sanyo obele**[1]. Female Kegite runs across the stage, in a disturbed state, from among the audience)*

KEGITE: My guy! My guy! Where is my guy? My boy friend, my sweetheart, my everything? Oh where are you, my honey, oh my God.

LOVER: *(Emerges from back stage)* Omo na me bi dis. If I see you from far away, my heart dey *gigi gigi gbam gbam*. Hey, chest me one time, *omo gbemi saya (Orchestra continues the song with the lover-Kegites as other Kegites come on stage from back-stage. Kegites' rhythms tumble as the party gets bluer and bluer.*

*This is followed by **Agbara elemu po**[2]. They dance round, sharing and drinking palm-wine from palm-wine calabashes and feeling light and high).*

KEGITE: I wan to jabo — collapse one time.
ALL: Jabo. Fall flat on one opeke, damsel.
KEGITE: I wan to sewere — go crazy for love.
ALL: Sewere — lose your mind straight.
KEGITE: I want to pepe — hook one better hip!
ALL: Pepe — catch a slender!

*(The palm-wine session hits a climax and the songs **Emu o emu o gbemi saya omoge**[3], **Everybody gyrate oh**[4] and **I see one boy**[5] reel on. The Kegites' dance attains a frenzied peak as they dance towards down stage right. They cluster and freeze. Immediately, cultists emerge from backstage in dreadful outfits carrying cutlasses, axes and other lethal objects.*

CULTIST: Couchi couchi.
ALL: Hey!
CULTIST: Couchi couchi.
ALL: Hey!!
CULTIST: Couchi couchi.
ALL: He eey hey!!!.

*(They sing an unintelligible number; **Na na na na**[6] and dance round their leader and freeze at the centre stage. Immediately, a University girl and her sugar-*

daddy emerge from the audience holding hands. A Porter gazes at them from a distance).

CHIEF: Baby, baby.
BABY: Chief, chief!
CHIEF: Baby, baby.
BABY: Na mi be dat *(She turns round for him to admire her).*
CHIEF: Baby. Okay, I go see you later *(He turns to leave as the lady runs after him).*
BABY: No way, Chief. Come and see me now. You have not settled me. Oya, settle me now, now. You think say na free service? *(Turning red and ferocious. Chief gets the message).*
CHIEF: Okay, com take, wetin? *(He dips his hand into his pocket and brings out some money).*
BABY: Na now you sabi. Thank you chief *(Porter pushes her back as she makes to pass him by).*
PORTER: Go back, go back I say! Where you dey come from self?
BABY: Ah ah, Mr Porter which one be your own?
PORTER: University campus girl just dey come back at 2:30a.m., and you think say I, my very self, Mr Ben the Porter, you

	think say I go allow you enter hostel, just like dat? No way! Go back.
BABY:	Are you my parent? Better mind your business and leave me alone. *(She tries again to pass him by, but he pushes her back and she falls).*
PORTER:	I say go back, you no dey hear word? Wetin you take me for? I must do my job o.
BABY:	Mind yourself, Mr Porter.
PORTER:	I say go back.
BABY:	*(She does a quick re-think and gets the cue.)* Okay, I know your problem. *(She turns her back to him and removes some money from her purse)* Take! Take!!
PORTER:	Hen eh, na now you dey begin talk. *(He collects the money from her.)* Why you con dey act as if you no know the formula before, before. Okay enter now *(He steps aside for her)* good girl. *(She dimps and passes through the stage to the back stage checking her makeup and dress, walking to down stage left. She passes by four girls with whom she exchanges pleasantries. The girls come to down stage left).*

GIRL 1: Sandy baby, I dey feel you.
GIRL 2: You dey feel me?
OTHER GIRLS: We dey feel you.
GIRL 2: Me I get plenty things to yarn oh, una wan hear?
OTHER GIRLS: Yarn us now.
GIRL 2: That man yesterday, I flabbergasted him.
OTHER GIRLS: We trust you.
GIRL 2: I took him to the right.
ALL: Kere wawa *(They all turn to the right and shake their buttocks)*.
GIRL 2: To the left.
ALL: Kere wawa *(They turn left and also shake their buttocks)*.
GIRL 2: To the middle.
ALL: Kere wawawa *(Similar action is performed down-stage)*.
GIRL 2: As if that one no do me. I come take am to heaven, from heaven to the earth. From earth down to hell again.
ALL: Chickolo *(They freeze as light beams on them and comes on fully on down stage. Alhaji Mai-Kudi emerges from the audience and walks towards Mr Ben)*.
ALHAJI: Mr Ben, Mr Ben.

PORTER:	Ah, Alhaji Maikudi.
ALHAJI:	How are you today?
PORTER:	I'm fine.
ALHAJI:	How is work?
PORTER:	We thank God.
ALHAJI:	You see I'm very happy today, walahi; you see, I just won a contract in Abuja.
PORTER:	Na big big money be dat.
ALHAJI:	Yes, big money. I want to spend my money with beautiful beautiful girls. I wan make you helf me get two beautiful girls.
PORTER:	Alhaji. Dem no dey sam sam, at all at all.
ALHAJI:	Ah ah! Mr Ben.
PORTER:	Alhaji I say dem no dey. Them dey serve siesta, you know, night sleep.
ALHAJI:	Ah ah Mr Ben. Okay, I know what is wrong. Here. Have this for your kola *(Alhaji gives him some money)*.
PORTER:	Ah! Dem dey, Alhaji. Dem dey. You sey two girls, abi? Just two? *(Alhaji affirms by shaking his head)*. Okay I dey come *(He runs on stage and knocks)*.
GIRLS:	Na who be dat now? Na sakara male or na Mr Porter?
PORTER:	Announcing Mr Ben, the Porter.

GIRLS:	Hei hei *(jumping with excitement and advertising their bodily wares in their shapes and sizes).*
PORTER:	Hey hei, sh sh shut up. I need two beautiful girls.
GIRL 1:	*(Jumps forward)* Mr Porter, see me now. Jugs lomo!
GIRL 2:	*(Pushes her aside.)* Commot. Mr Porter. Look at me. Tooth pick, slender-slender, lepa lomo!!
GIRL 3:	I beg sit o, find somewhere sit down. Mr Porter, take a good look at me. Puff — puff, orobo lomo!!!
GIRL 4:	Oh oh, Mr Porter shine your face well-well. Now, see. Hip-star, randy ass lomo!!!
PORTER:	Ehn. Thank you all. I know wetin I want. Hem, em. *(They all rush at him shouting and hustling to be picked)* You and you *(He picks two girls).* The great and rich Alhaji Maikudi is around.
GIRLS:	Hei, today is our lucky day. *(The two girls follow the Porter)*
GIRL 3:	Ah Shade, temi bami. I am done for. They don leave us go again. I don spend my registration money finish...

GIRL 4:	Ah! registration money? Your own small. Where I go get money for hand-outs?
Both:	Eh! registration and hand-out money!!
PORTER:	Alhaji, here they are.
ALHAJI:	*(Admiring the girls)* Thank you Mr Ben, let's go, girls. *(They leave).*

*(Light beams on them as drums accompany the narrator on stage. The narrator emerges from the audience; he encourages active participation from the audience as they sing **Egbe ti a se**[7] over and over again. Repeat as many times as possible and encourage the audience to join).*

NARRATOR:	All right, Ladies and Gentlemen.
AUDIENCE:	Yes.
NARRATOR:	It is quite unfortunate, yes quite unfortunate. Parents sent you to the University to learn *(He walks towards the girls)* but, alas, you have turned yourself to aristo babes. You have glamourised prostitution on our campuses by selling your body to the highest bidder. Get down from my stage, will you get down from my stage at once?
GIRLS:	Wetin dey do you. Na your body sef? Na we get our body? *(They hiss and walk out).*

NARRATOR: And what do we have here? *(He turns to the cultists)* Muslims and Christians from decent backgrounds but unfortunately, they have turned themselves into cultists; raping, looting, and killing innocent students. This is the peak of societal degeneration. Get down from my stage, will you? Get down from my stage. *(They glare at him menacingly as they leave the stage. He now moves to the Kegites.)* Gone are the days, Ladies and Gentlemen, when University Kegites used to be University Kegites; but the bunch of Kegites we have here are rotten and corrupt. They have turned their gyration venue to a sex abode. Get down from my stage. Now! *(They sing **sanyo sanyo** as they leave the stage. The orchestra sings **Egbe t'a a se** and rouses the audience. They sing it over and over until narrator cuts in)*

NARRATOR: Hm. Ladies and Gentlemen. What that song says is simple. It says that a group that you belong to, and from which you derive no benefit, you might as well quit it. Nothing untoward will befall you if you do. Indeed, there is another song more melodious which more aptly stresses that fact.

*(**Dark times are over?**[8] is picked by the orchestra and the narrator dances to the melody before cutting in.)*

But we better save it till the end, for those who persevere. Till then *(He paces up and down to gain attention)*. Yes, Ladies and Gentlemen, when I was growing up a short while ago, our elders used to enrich their discussions with parables and proverbs. For instance, kola-nut. They say that we eat kola-nut for pleasure. But when kola-nut visits our teeth with decay and plaque, don't we flee from it like a plague?

AUDIENCE: Beeni. It is so indeed.
NARRATOR: I can't hear you loud enough.
AUDIENCE: Beeni. We say na so.
NARRATOR: That is what that song is saying, my dear friends. What is happening to our campuses these days? The whole nation is worried, and you know rumour spreads faster than wild bush fire. They say our campuses have become dens of

terror, like life in the shadow of death. All over, in the newspapers, on the radios and television, it is rumours galore. What are they saying? They say that nobody, not even the students who used to consider themselves lords and ladies on their campuses, dare go out, dare walk on their own campuses, anytime from six-o'clock in the evening. Tell me, all of you. Can this be true? *(He asks the audience as he paces further to arrest their attention.)*

AUDIENCE: Beeni, yes oo!

NARRATOR: En, what has happened to the love gardens, the theatre halls, which came alive only at night? All these propositions that become enduring: serious love and social issues, have become terror tales? I hear our love gardens on campuses have become shallow graves. Tell me. Is it true?

AUDIENCE: Beeni o. Na so we see am ooh!!

NARRATOR: *(He paces faster and more agitated to further arrest the attention of the audience.)* Please, let's discuss it. Let's weave the story up and act it like a play and explain it to ourselves. May be, somehow, through that process, a solution will emerge, wherein our campuses can regain their original freedom which makes them the envy of the whole society all over the world. We come to the University to learn, gain exposure to the world, don't we? Ehen. Our parents suffer so much to get us to qualify for admission. Thousands of naira to get us to sit and pass WASSCE, SSCE or GCE and UME, without which nobody can step into what we used to call the Ivory Tower. Yes, we qualify, but it does not mean automatic admission. We know, don't we? that hundreds of thousands make the cut-off point of entry, but less than tens of thousands secure admissions, isn't it? Ladies and Gentlemen, our proud parents come here to celebrate our good luck when we join the lucky ones who gain admission to the University.

(A young lady in jeans rushes out from the audience and interrupts him, with an American falsetto accent.)

LADY: Hei, stop it men! Stop the campaign okay! What's the point, men? You a preacher or somering? What's all this politics going on here then?

NARRATOR: Take it easy, my dear lady, and please listen. I am just exchanging views with all these people here. After all, Shakespeare says the world's a stage...

LADY: Oh, you, a clown or somering? You wanna put up a show then?

NARRATOR: Well, yes. We might as well put up a show, if that will help me make my point. After all, theatre creates the illusion of men and women actually living and breathing before an audience's very eyes...

LADY: Cut it okay. You, a scholar or somering? Always getting on with them long long theory; get on with the play then. What's the subject anyway? I could do with a show than them boring lectures, okay.

NARRATOR: *(Exasperated and winks at the audience, courting their sympathy.)* See me see trouble. Well, as I was just saying, let's discuss the story of our campuses, like an exchange in the theatre.

(Turns to the lady) Okay, em, excuse me miss... em what's your name miss?

LADY:	I don't miss nothing. I am Beatrice, simple.
NARRATOR:	Yes, Beatrice. What a beautiful name. We can make a play out of it, because it sounds so serious. What's going on? But join this song first while we get other actors. *(He starts **Bo wo lu ni ko le pani**[9], rousing Beatrice and the audience to join. He moves inside the audience seeking actors.)* It is like keeping a bad company which does no one any good. We run away from it like one quits the company of a leper. Let's get on with the play. Yes, from that angle, is there anyone willing to act one role or the other? ...Yes, feel free to come out, don't be shy now... *(Hands begin to shoot up and catcalls follow spontaneously. He invites them one by one unto the arena).*
	Yes, Ladies and Gentlemen, we are getting there gradually. Sooner or later, the stammerer will call his father's name. Just yesterday, as the rumour goes, they said a University girl was gang-raped, in broad daylight, just like that.
AUDIENCE:	Just like that?

NARRATOR: At about 4.pm. Can you believe that... Well, you take up that role. Who were these sadistic characters? They say it was for nothing. Just to prove they have power. Well, let's have two people, two rugged people, daring enough to do such a thing, just to prove they have power. Yes, you *(pointing at two ferocious looking guys)* both of you look rugged and strong enough to act the roles. Yes, your looks are sufficiently ferocious to pass for such characters.
CULTIST: Zongwe
AUDIENCE: Eh
CULTIST: Zongwe
AUDIENCE: Eh
CULTIST: Eh eh
AUDIENCE: Eh eh *(Guys run up stage and push narrator off)*
NARRATOR: Take it easy, ehn. It is only a play, yes, thank you. Em, we need more people, to lead some other groups. The Christian Union and the Moslem Students Society *(Volunteers come out, with religious choruses which they encourage the audience to join: **Igbala ofe lamu wa**[10], **Isilamu ko ni tu**[11].*

The narrator continues his recruitment).
Yes now, a representative of the Jaycee and Man O' War. Yes come out.

MAN O' WAR: Trust Man O'War. Wee!

AUDIENCE: Waa!

*(They sing **Ewa na jem se**[12] and jog on stage and **Another challenge o**[13] to usher the Jaycee in)*

NARRATOR: Ladies and Gentlemen.

AUDIENCE: Yes.

NARRATOR: Fellow Compatriots of this land of Odaju.

AUDIENCE: Yes.

NARRATOR: So what am I still waiting for? The cast is now complete. Enjoy the play *(He leaves).*

BEATRICE: *(Just raped. The lady screams from back stage, resulting in a commotion on stage as people run helter-skelter. Two cultists emerge from back stage, pause for a while, set down some stolen items to zip up their trousers, pick the items up again and then bounce off the stage.)*

Yee! Yeee!! Egba mi. I don die. I am ruined. My life is finished.

They have destroyed my life ooo! *(She collapses, writhing in pain and hysteria.)*

CHRISTIAN SISTER 1: Take it easy. The Lord shall take control in Jesus name.
ALL: Amen? (*She ignores them and continues in her hysteria.*)
CHRISTIAN SISTER 2: My sister in the Lord, what happened?
BEATRICE: They have ruined my life, those evil bastards. They invited me to join their club. I thought it was a godly, open club. Now see my predicament... Oh! my God.
MOSLEM BROTHER 1: Allahu akbar. God is great. Leave it for Allah. But first, tell us. What happened? What did they do to you?
BEATRICE: I can't say. I can't tell you. Can't you see for yourself?
(*Gesturing her lower region.*)
MOSLEM BROTHER 2: Subhanallahi. We can see allright. But these people who did this to you. Who are they?
BEATRICE: No no no, I can't tell you who they are. Leave that one. They'll kill me. Ha! Those people. Hm. They say even if I am in the bedroom of an Army General, **they'll fish me out and pluck out my eyes,** before they shoot me dead. No, I can't tell you. Those devils have done their worst. Let's leave it like that. I don't want to die.

CHRISTIAN SISTER 1: My sister in Christ. Do not cover the truth. Tell the truth and the truth will make you whole. They can't touch your soul.

BEATRICE: Well, they have destroyed my body, my life, my everything, oh nooo!

CHRISTIAN SISTER 3: Fear not those who can kill the body, but can't touch the spirit.

MOSLEM BROTHER 3: Awuzubillahi. May Allah and His prophet save us. Give us their names and we shall flush them out with a few verses. Just tell us the truth, Allah, we'll finish them. Just tell us the truth.

BEATRICE: Please forget it. It is all my fate, my destiny. I don't want to worsen my misery. I cannot even tell my parents. Oh, those bastards... with all that blood, all that thick smell of alcohol mixed with blood... that smelly concoction of spirit and smoke. Oh horrible, horrible. (*Evidently scared stiff and still hysterical.*) Ah! they are here, see them. They are there, everywhere. Please leave me alone. Leave them alone. They are so powerful. Please let me bury my head in shame. But I don't want to die. They have vowed to kill me, if I tell. They will, I know.

MAN O' WAR & JAYCEE: *(They both enter.)* What's the problem? What's going on here?

CHRISTIAN SISTER 2: Don't worry. God has taken control.

MAN O' WAR: Control of what? Tell us, we will mobilize the forces on the ground to deal with it. Trust Man O' War. Wee. Waa!!

JAYCEE: With confidence in humanity, the philanthropic spirit of good people, all evil forces will be relegated. Love will overcome. So, tell us those responsible for spreading tears, sorrow and blood. We have contacts, locally, nationally and internationally, to combat evil forces.
*(Suddenly, there is an outburst of screams and Beatrice collapses. Speaking in tongues, the Christian sisters and Moslem brothers pray and **Elimi loruko awon ogun orun**[14] and **Lai la ila la**[15] fervently in succession as they surround her to revive her.)*

MAN O' WAR: Well. This is the beginning of the end of dark days in our midst. Those whose trade-mark is terror and blood must be routed.

JAYCEE: Ultimately, humanity, freedom and love must triumph over tears and fear, and those who trade in evil.

MAN O' WAR: The die is cast.

JAYCEE: Dark days must be truly over. *(On that note of resolve, they carry Beatrice out as the Christian and Moslem brethren sing out of stage).*

End of Scene One

SCENE TWO

(The scene change must be rapid with no time lapse. Create a new setting before the audience).

NARRATOR: Well, dear audience. Horrible, isn't it? A total outrage, what goes on in our campuses these days. In the past, as many of you know, our campuses used to be safe havens, where freedom bred and blossomed. No, not anymore. They have vandalized the purity and pride of that young and innocent girl. In other circumstances, there is brutal physical assault of deadly proportions. They are omnipotent. She dares not reveal the identity of her destroyers and assailants... But, wait a minute *(A song is heard)*. I hear horrible noises over there. Let's hide and watch.
Hi loi loi la la hi lo[16]

YEPA 1: Couchi couchi.

CULTIST:	Heh!
YEPA 1:	Couchi couchi.
CULTIST:	Heh!
YEPA:	Couchi couchi.
CULTIST:	Heh he!

CULTIST: *Hi loi la la hi lo*
(They begin to dance round in frenzied movements raising their axes and cutlasses up in the air. As they settle down for a joint...)

YEPA 1: When birds hoot at night, we know that the winged spirit forages the sky.

YEPA 2: When snakes hiss at night all chickens vanish into hiding.

CULTIST 1: Like a dog trapped in the lion's den, those who join us are in big trouble.

CULTIST 2: Yes, those who oppose us are in hell.

CULTIST 3: And those who denounce us roast in fire.

CULTISTS 4 & 5: We are the omnipotent.

ALL: We of the underworld commune!
Hi loi loi lala hi lo... *(They all take their space sitting round the fire.)*

YEPA 2: Owner of wings of the world. Did you enjoy it? I mean that young, succulent and juicy one. Ha! I was in cloud ten. It was bad coming back to this world after being within those ridges and thighs. Ah! Did you behold those teasing nipples?

YEPA 1: There was no need to look. That was why I pushed you off as you were so gentle with her. Hey. Ah! What is power? What is fulfilment if you begin to give in to emotion and pity? Your business was to dig hard and subdue. (*Pulling harder at the hemp stick and flexing his sinews.*) Yes man. Ultimate power; power to seduce, power to kill, power to frighten those who claim to have knowledge, power to threaten those grey-headed teachers out of their labs and cool offices, power to change the marks or force them to award grades.

YEPA 2: Yes man, ultimate power for four or five of us to mount a single butter-eating babe. Power to subdue spoilt children who are inheriting looted wealth. Force them to submit their money and their smooth bodies.

YEPA 1: Couchi couchi.
ALL: Eh!
YEPA 1: Couchi couchi.
ALL: Eh!
YEPA 1: Couchi couchi.
ALL: Ehh eh!
(Bursting into a song)
Na we dey rule o[17]

More dance and songs. Meanwhile, Man O'War leader has led in the police to their location very stealthily.)

MAN O' WAR: Officers, Officers, we are close to the place, listen.
(Songs are heard from a distance.)

OFFICER: Now listen, as soon as *Omo Awo* goes in. I mean as soon as the Man O' War leader goes in, we attack immediately. Do you understand?

OTHER MEN: Yes sir.

MAN O' WAR: *(Coughs)* Yee pa!

YEPA 1: Pa ripa o. Who goes there?

YEPA 2: Is it a bush rat jumping out of the hole at noon?

MAN O' WAR: No, only the initiates see one another. You doubt me, not so? It is well, snakes hiss, winged-spirit ride in the dark. I am *omo awo*.

YEPA 1 & 2: *Omo awo*, couchi couchi.

MAN O' WAR: Eh!

YEPA 1 & 2: Couchi couchi.

MAN O' WAR: Eh!

YEPA 1 & 2: Couchi couchi.

MAN O' WAR: Ehh eh!

YEPA 2: Then relax and join us. What kept you and others so late? We were almost

	winding up. And one needs to catch some sleep before day-break.

YEPA 1: Where are the rest? The commune was so slim tonight.

MAN O' WAR: Which rest? The ones you raped or the ones you shot, half-dead? Which?

YEPA 1: Ha hn hn! What kind of talk is this? Or you're merely being jealous? Anyway, we merely obliged her and fulfilled her request.

MAN O' WAR: No. You destroyed her essence, her dream and her pride. That's what you did. That's what you've always done with her type.

YEPA 2: Shut up! What has come over you? What trifle is that? How can an *awo* talk like this?

YEPA 1: We mated with her spirit to give her courage and power over her mates and her rivals. She will never experience fear again in her life.

MAN O' WAR: *(Smiling)* Hm. You both amuse me. A girl came to the University to learn. You cornered her and took her pride away from her. You destroyed the moral base of her existence.

ALL: *(Awareness dawns)* What, who are you? Impostor, traitor?
You die. *(They make to attack him but he faces up to them with Judoka gestures. The police appear and there are gunshots. One or two are mortally wounded, some escape.)*

MAN O' WAR: Give up. The game is up. It is time for reckoning.

POLICE: Put your hands above your heads and don't try anything funny or you are stone dead. You have killed enough. Time is up for your kind in our institutions of higher learning.

YEPA 1: *(Quivering and frightened).* Oh no sir. Emm. We are innocent. I mean I am innocent, sir. Believe me sir. It is the devil sir.

POLICE: Shut up or you shall explain yourself in the other world.

YEPA 1: No sir, em... yes sir. It is true. It is devil, sir. My mother's rivals are after me. It is so sir.

YEPA 2: Shut up. You wretched worm. Ultimate power knows no fear. Not even death is bold enough... *(Man O' War lands a karate wedge on his neck. He falls, but goes on.)* Not even death can conquer ultimate power. We shall go on like the world goes on.

POLICE: Okay now. You'll tell the story of your ultimate power in the grave. Death is the instant penalty for people like you who wreak terror on our campuses. I can't wait to waste you. Officers, get them in a single file and move them out. *(They are pushed roughly out of the stage as the orchestra resonates the Bad Company rhythm, **Egbe ti a se**.)*

End of Scene Two

SCENE THREE

(Lights come on a court scene with the necessary paraphernalia of a law court and a huge cardboard with 'LAW COURT' conspicuously displayed. Narrator dances in and arranges the court, placing the cardboard on which 'LAW COURT' is conspicuously displayed, on the wall. Others dance in to help him arrange chairs. They dance out as soon as they are through, leaving the narrator on the stage.)

MEMBER OF THE AUDIENCE 1: Mr Narrator.
NARRATOR: Yes.
MEMBER OF THE AUDIENCE 1: Can you please tell this honourable audience what will happen to Yepa 1 and his group now that they have been arrested.
NARRATOR: Just wait and see.
MEMBER OF THE AUDIENCE 2: Mr Narrator.
NARRATOR: Yes.
MEMBER OF THE AUDIENCE 2: Rumour has it that Yepa 1 and his group are bribing some members of the judiciary; is this true?

NARRATOR: Just wait and see.
MEMBER OF THE AUDIENCE 3: Sit down young man. I say sit down. Not all members of the judiciary are corrupt or Mr Narrator am I wrong?
NARRATOR: Just wait and see.
MEMBER OF THE AUDIENCE 4: Mr Narrator, has the play ended? We are yearning for more action.
*(The orchestra raises a song **Eyin alapa ma sise**[18]. Court audience comes on stage. They all sit until the Clerk announces the arrival of the judge. After three knocks are heard with the call to order, everybody rises after the pronouncement 'court'. No one sits down until the judge is well seated. The clerk rises again to call the next case for hearing.)*

JUDGE: Call the first case of the day.
CLERK: The only case in today's sitting is case No. 05 /7410230. Yepa 1 versus the State. (***Yepa 1*** *is brought in by the police. He is made to enter the box. The prosecuting lawyer and incidentally the only lawyer in the court introduces himself as the one standing in for the State. Then the clerk reads out the charges against **Yepa 1**.)*

Prosecutor: I am Barrister Williams defending the state.

Clerk: Yepa 1, you are accused of raping an innocent girl on 16.05.2005 *(the date can be changed to suit each production)*, robbing law abiding citizens of their valuable possessions, engaging in violent killings, and disrupting the peace on the same said day.

Judge: Has the accused not availed himself of the right of a defence counsel?

Yepa 1: No your lordship, I need no lawyer to defend me. My case is simple and straightforward. Besides, I cannot pay the bill.

Judge: Alright then, proceed with the prosecution.

Prosecutor: Yepa 1, answer to the three charges levelled against you: *Inter alia;* raping, looting and breaching the peace. Are you guilty or not guilty?

Yepa 1: This must be a practical joke. You must have rehearsed your lines in this concluding sequence of this make-belief drama very well. What have you just said about peace and security? In this city of Odaju where it is those who instruct the thief to steal that call the attention of the farm-owner to keep vigil?

PROSECUTOR: I object to this digression, my lord. The accused person cannot be allowed to frustrate this court or deride the noble objective of the good citizens of the city to cleanse it of hoodlums and criminals.

JUDGE: Objection upheld. I warn you, Mr Yepa. Go straight and simply answer the question, since you refuse to engage the services of a lawyer. If you continue your evasive game, you may be charged for Contempt of the Court.

YEPA 1 (*Derisively*) My lord, I state again that I don't need a lawyer. I can not afford the exorbitant prices, not after the ceasure of the pre-election security votes that we used to share in order to run a life of luxury, like the rest of you.

PROSECUTOR: Objection, my lord. You cannot allow such unruly behaviour from a criminal.

YEPA 1: Did you hear him call me a criminal already? The judgement must have been passed, outside of this court then. (*There is murmuring from the court audience.*)

CLERK: (*Rises and shouts*) Order!!!

JUDGE:	Objection upheld. (*To Yepa I*) Go straight to your points. Do not provoke this court to take a drastic action that you will regret.
YEPA 1:	Alright: I will try to answer the question as briefly as possible. Of course, I am not guilty. I only partook in the general game of survival in Odaju land. Since Olorioko, the former dictator of the Republic of Odaju land, laid us off after the elections, we the ex-recruits need to continue to survive since our masquerade can no longer dance to silent drums. (*Light dims as actors freeze on stage. It comes fully on down stage. Area boys emerge from the audience praising their political godfather*).
AREA 1:	Shua! Baba able. A-B-L-E, baba ever.
AREA 2:	Baba tiyin lama se ku se e. We go serve you till we die.
AREA 3:	Baba ani eti poju, you are too much.
AREA 4:	Odaju father.
GODFATHER:	Look. You guys. The game is over.
AREA BOYS:	Ah! What game?
GODFATHER:	I am no longer in government. The baton has changed hands.

AREA 3: Nothing dey happen baba.
GODFATHER: You guys have to look for other means of survival. No more windfalls.
AREA 2: That one go hard to do o, what will happen to us?
(Godfather brings out a pistol from his pocket.)
GODFATHER: Eyin guys. You have to go out there and use your brains, now.
AREA BOYS: Ah *(Realising the meaning)* Na wa! Odaju land don pafuka! Katakata don burst. *(They all come together.)*
AREA 1: Eyin guys, we shall terrorise Odaju land. Father, you will hear from us soon. Guys let's go. *(Light goes back fully on stage.)*
COURT AUDIENCE: *(A lot of murmuring in the courtroom.)* Students turning into Area Boys! Ah, what a country!!
CLERK: Order!
YEPA 1: *(He continues)* We took to the roads to collect the shares that are no more forthcoming. Am I totally to blame? My actions were compelled by poverty and the need to survive.
COURT AUDIENCE: Enu ti gboro – he has developed high taste.

CLERK: *(Rises and shouts)* Order!!!

YEPA 1: As for the rape *(To the theatre audience)*, you all saw how she dressed or undressed? Barely enough to cover the teasing parts.*(Beatrice walks past and members of the audience whistle at her.)* What man can resist that? We were all moved except those who were cowardly or frigid. I am as guilty as the parents and the permissive society which allow such open acts of sexual harassment.

PROSECUTOR: Objection my lord! Is this lunatic going to be allowed to continue his ranting? He is just begging the issue and making lousy and untenable excuses.

JUDGE: You are abusing the privilege of democracy that grants freedom of speech. Sum up in the next few minutes or else....

YEPA 1: My lord, I will hasten up my submissions, not minding the bias.

COURT AUDIENCE: The bias? Which bias?

YEPA 1: Yes, it surprises me that I am the only accused person in court, in spite of the fact that my close associate, Yepa 2, was equally arrested.*(Lights dim on actors as they freeze and come fully on down stage. Judge comes in from the right door dressed gorgeously in traditional attire.)*

JUDGE: Impossible, extremely impossible. I can't allow this to happen. I wield a lot of influence in this land to be able to sway matters in my favour. I have money. I can do and undo in this country. A whole Judge, to be rubbished, just like that? Legs will advise eyes that will not fall on evil days. No way. *(Stage is set in a corner for the D P O who is seated.)*

CORPORAL: Good afternoon madam.

JUDGE: Good day, Officer. I'm from the High Court of Justice of Odaju land.

CORPORAL: You must be em...

JUDGE: Justice Komolafe, yes.

CORPORAL: Oh yes Justice Komolafe, you're welcome madam.

JUDGE: Please I'd like to see the DPO.

CORPORAL: Hold on madam. *(Walks to the DPO and salutes.)* Sir, Justice Komolafe is here to see you.

DPO: Let her in.

CORPORAL: Yes sir. *(He salutes again, then approaches the Judge.)* You may go in madam.

JUDGE: Here. Have this for your lunch. *(He collects it from behind, with eagerness.)*

CORPORAL: Thank you madam. Thank you and God bless.

JUDGE: *(Enters the DPO's office)* My DPO.

DPO: The Justice herself. What brings you here today?

JUDGE: Nothing much. It is just a little problem I want you to help me solve.

DPO: You mean Justices do have problems too?

JUDGE: Oh just one of those things. My enemies are at work. They are working hard to tarnish my image — ruin my reputation built over thirty years.

DPO: Well, why don't you have a seat so that we can discuss better.

JUDGE: Thank you. You see, there is this nephew of mine in your custody.

DPO: Our custody? What has he done?

JUDGE: Well, you see, he is innocent o! He has not committed any crime. He was just unfortunate to get rounded up with

	these rogues and hooligans we have around. He is very innocent, I can assure you.
DPO:	But madam you are a Justice yourself and you know how the law operates.
JUDGE:	Yes, and because I am a Justice, that poor boy must not go to jail. Em. DPO. And as you know, it is the design of the evil ones, enemies of progress. They wish to exploit this little matter, this small error of my little nephew, to undo me. Please, DPO. Don't let them. You will not regret this favour. Here is one million naira, specially packaged for you. Just a little token to start with. *(she puts a bag of money on his table.)*
DPO:	But madam, you know this is too small. There are too many mouths to shut. This is just too small. You know how things are. Just too many ears to block up there.
JUDGE:	Well, my DPO just do it for me. After carrying out the assignment, I promise to compensate you. And make room for all those ones up there. Not to worry.
DPO:	All right then, I'll see what I can do about the release of your nephew, today.

JUDGE:	My DPO, I know I can always count on you.
DPO:	Consider it done madam; have a nice day.
JUDGE:	Thank you DPO. *(She walks away.)* Officer, bye bye.
CORPORAL:	No objection my lord oh. Thank you at all at all o. Bye bye o!
DPO:	Officer Bako.
CORPORAL:	Sir.
DPO:	Go to the Criminal Investigation Division and tell the officer-in-charge that I want that Komolafe of a boy released immediately, okay. And tell him to see me immediately after.
CORPORAL:	Yes sir.
	(Light dims and comes fully back on stage. The judge is apparently uncomfortable. She wipes her forehead with her handkerchief as the court audience exclaims 'ha'.)
YEPA 1:	*(Grinning)* I learnt reliably that he was flown out of the country yesterday, courtesy of the police and, his aunt, the honorable judge, here seated.
JUDGE:	*(Summons courage).* Enough of this nonsense! You are truly insane!! *(To the police)* He is a mental case, fit only for

	an asylum. When he regains his sanity, the prosecutor will notify the court. Appropriate ruling will then be made. I therefore adjourn this case. Take him back to the cell. *(The Judge, the clerk, and the prosecutor leave the court.)*
YEPA 1:	*(To the court audience)* What else do you expect? Do I sound or look like a lunatic? *(The audience makes various disapproving remarks over the conclusion of the case.)*
OFFICER:	Officers, take Yepa 1 back to the prison.
NARRATOR:	*(Steps out as a police officer forcefully grips Yepa 1)* Hold it, hold it everyone. No one is going to prison yet. We all are here to determine who is guilty. *(To the audience)* Ladies and Gentlemen, is there a clear case of injustice or is it a fair judgement? It appears we all seem dissatisfied. I propose we conduct an open people's court to adjudicate on the matter. Let's all be seated while we mandate a member of the audience to be the judge—the people's judge.
MEMBER OF THE AUDIENCE 1:	Agbe! Agbe!! Agbe!!!

(The audience unanimously agrees and

Agbe is carried on stage and some members of the audience follow him dancing and shouting his name. Simultaneously, the inscription 'COURT OF LAW' is removed and replaced with 'PEOPLE'S COURT'. Agbe is given a robe which he rejects as he occupies the judge's seat; but he soon stands up.)

AGBE: Ladies and Gentlemen, I thank you for electing me unanimously. It may surprise you that I rejected the robe. It is a rejection of a legal system that is marred with technicalities and hypocrisy. Our court of law in Odaju land is an appendage to the larger rotten system out there. It is a place justice has been sold for a mesh of porridge by a rotten, corrupt and nepotic leadership. Now, to the main business of the day. *(He clears his throat.)* No doubt, Yepa 1 is guilty.

COURT AUDIENCE 1: He is a killer.

COURT AUDIENCE 2: A rapist.

COURT AUDIENCE 3: And a cultist.

AGBE: Yes he is guilty and I'm happy he has never denied it for once. Our elders say the *elulu* bird that invites rain should be beaten by the same rain. To start with, what do we do with Yepa, if I may throw the matter back to all of you?

MEMBER OF THE AUDIENCE 2: Jail him.

MEMBER OF THE AUDIENCE 3: Kill him.

MEMBER OF THE AUDIENCE 4: Send him to a rehabilitation centre.

MEMBER OF THE AUDIENCE 5: Castrate him, so that pretty girls might walk in the streets in peace.

AGBE: Ladies and Gentlemen, rogues and vagabonds like Yepa continue to brandish their weapons to terrorize the society, which condemns them to poverty and squalor. It is laudable to rid our society of rogues like Yepa, but is there justice, if two separate laws are erected in the society, one set of laws for the poor and the hungry; children of the poorly paid workers, the unemployed and unrewarded hewers of wood and carriers of water? Those laws keep the poor down and weaken his resolve to be upright and decent. He is open to temptation through frustration and despair. He is consigned by our unjust society to poverty, crime and cultism. What other options are there for a student who manages to pay fees and passes exams but cannot feed himself? What options exist for an army of university and polytechnic graduates who have no jobs to go into? They become armed robbers, insensitive killers in a bid to survive. In the end, they get caught and the law takes its toll on them. The other set of law is made for the rich and opulent, the real robbers who with a stroke of the pen or the power of the gun command billions of dollars into their foreign accounts. Yes, Yepa is guilty, so are all those who perpetrate social injustice in our land. We look forward to a day when our land will be rid of these factors that make rape, cultism and violence necessary. That day the Yepas of this world will cease to exist and the dark times will truly be over. Henceforth, everyone should be treated equally before the law, if we really crave for peace and security of lives and property. Therefore, all those alleged to have committed any offence or act as an accomplice must appear in court to defend themselves even if it is Olorioko himself.

COURT AUDIENCE 3: Haba. This is impossible. There are limits. Olorioko has immunity. He has the Constitution in his favour. He cannot be subjected to humiliation like ordinary mortals.

AGBE: All such favours and privileges must go. The President is a citizen and must be subjected to the dictates of the law, like all other citizens. Excesses must be punished. I heard the other day that the Vice-President of a neighbouring country was de-robed, for allegations of corrupt practices.

COURT AUDIENCE 2: Just like that? *O tio*. No way. It cannot happen in this our Odaju land.

COURT AUDIENCE 1: His entire clan will wage a bitter war in his defence.

AGBE: *(With emphasis)* Well, it can and it will. Also, no exercise of personal rights should be provocative as to tempt or infringe on others' rights. Lastly, all provocative dresses are hereby banned in public places. *(Identifies a court* *audience scantly and skimpily dressed and ushers her out of the court.)* Ladies and Gentlemen, no doubt, Yepa 1 is a product of the system that needs complete overhauling, to avoid the breeding of numerous Yepas. Our case is similar to that of a man with a crooked leg. You condemn him that his load is tilted. It is not his fault, the whole structure is responsible.

COURT AUDIENCE 1: The whole structure is responsible.

ALL: Agbe!

AGBE: Ladies and Gentlemen, we are in a democratic era, this is the people's court and you are the people, I can deduce from the majority that you want Yepa 1 to be taken to an institution where he can be reformed. So you and you, *(Pointing to the policemen)* take him. Yepa 1 is hereby sentenced to 21 years in prison.

COURT AUDIENCE 2: Yes! *(They all rejoice.)* Yes o. That is the least punishment he can get.

AGBE: Ladies and Gentlemen, we all must say no to cultism and all anti-social behaviours, so that dark times will truly be over. I rise!

ALL: Agbe... (*They all move, stand up to sing and dance. The orchestra joins in 'Dark Times Are Over?' as Agbe is lifted on proud shoulders.*)

Black-out

The End

SONGS

1. Sanyo sanyo obele/4x
   Awa le korin katun kawe wa, obele
   Awa le memu katun ka iwe wa, obele
   Sanyo sanyo obele/2x

Translation

Sanyo, sanyo, obele (4x)
We can sing and read our books,
We can booze and pass exams,
Sanyo, sanyo, obele (2x)

2. Agbara elemu po/2x
   O lana sori ope
   Ogbemu wa sile.

Translation

Mighty is the power of the tapster,
He cuts a path to the top of the palm-tree,
And fetches forth fresh palm-wine.

3. **Call:** Emu o, emu o gbemi saya omoge
   Res: Emu o emu o gbemi saya omoge

Translation

Dear old palmy
Land me straight in the bosom of a damsel.

4. Everybody gyrate oh, gyrate oh
   Everybody gyrate o gy gy gy gyrate.

5. I see one boy
   Soo
   He no wear pant
   Soo
   He no wear shirt
   Soo
   Bring am come here
   Soo soo eh
   O, Soo soo eh
   I say bring am
   Soo soo eh
   O, Soo soo eh

6. Na na na na na
   Na na na na na
   Na na na na na
   Na na na na na

7. Egbe ti ase tio gbe ni
   Aise re kole pani lara

Translation

A group we join
Which yields zero benefit,
If we quit it/no harm is done.

8. Dark times are Over
   A new day has come
   It's a new beginning
   The darkness is gone

9. Bowo luni kole pani/2x
   Igi ti a fehinti
   Tio gbani duro
   Bowo luni kole pani.

Translation

Feather weight tree,
Offers no support,
If it falls on you/it bears no effect.

10. Igbala ofe lamu wa
    Ti Jesu feje re se
    Igbala ofe lamu wa o
    Ewa gba igbala ofe o.

Translation

We bring forth free salvation
Ransomed with the blood of Jesus
Come, grab redemption/at no cost.

11. Isilamu koni tu
    Awa ta nse ao ni reyin
    Iwaju iwaju lao ma lo/lao ma lo
    Iwaju iwaju lao ma lo

Translation

Islam will not fall apart,
We devotees shall continue/to wax strong,
Forward, we shall march on,
Progress is our watch-word.

12. Ewa na jem se
    Eh jem se ewa
    Ewa tio lepo
    Ewa
    Ewa tio lata
    Ewa
    Ewa na jem se
    Eh jem se ewa

Translation

Boil it, boil the beans
Cook it to the boil
It has no oil,
It needs no pepper.
Boil the bean/till it is done.

13. Another challenge o/2x
    Another challenge o double double challenge o

14. Elimi loruko awon ogun orun o
    Elimi loruko awon malaika
    Ewa wo malaika to sese de/2x
    Moni lai lo
    Elo
    Elo elo elo elo
    Lai o elo

Translation

Hallo to the chorus of heavenly hosts
Exhort the name of all angels
Come, behold the new angel/that descends
Lai lo.

15. Lai la ila la/2x

16. Hi loi loi la la hi lo
Hi loi loi la la hilo lai lola/2x

17. Na we dey rule o/2x
If you go against us
I pity your mama

18. Eyin alapa ma sise
Eyin aje gboro dagba
Nigba to ba dojo ale
Fi aso ikoko bora.
Fire fire fire down below
Fire fire fire down below
Igba to ba dojo ale
Fi aso ikoko bora.

Translation

You idlers and loafers
You hooligans and vagabonds
When night falls
You clothe your backs/with hyena's skin
Fire, fire, fire down below (2x)
When night falls
You cloak yourself/in hyena's garment.